Who Is Jesus?

Written by Faytene Grasseschi
Illustrated by Michelle Vanderweir

Dedicated to
Keyanna-Joy Aviah Grasseschi
in celebration of her first Christmas.

Love,

Mom

This book belongs to:

_____

Jesus is so awesome.

My drawing about how awesome Jesus is:

Jesus is my best friend.

He stays beside me everywhere I go.

My drawing about how Jesus is my best friend:

Jesus is my healer.

He helps me whenever I am hurt.

My drawing about how Jesus is my healer:

He helps me whenever I am hurt

Jesus is my provider.

Everything I have comes from Him.

My drawing about how Jesus is my provider:

Jesus is my protector.

He shields me all the time.

My drawing about how Jesus is my protector:

Jesus is so strong.

He shows me how to be brave.

My drawing about how Jesus is so strong:

Jesus is my joy.

He fills my heart with so much happiness.

My drawing about how Jesus gives me joy:

Jesus is love.

Every good thing comes from Him.

My drawing about Jesus' love:

Jesus is my peace.

He fills my heart with so much comfort.

My drawing about Jesus' peace:

Jesus always listens.

He hears me when I call.

My drawing about how Jesus listens to me:

Jesus is my leader.

He guides me to the best places.

My drawing about Jesus being my leader:

Jesus is my helper.

He is always there when I need Him.

My drawing about how Jesus is my helper:

Jesus is very kind.

He always treats me so nice.

My drawing about how kind Jesus is:

Jesus is the smartest.

He knows the answer to every question.

My drawing about how Jesus is the smartest:

Jesus is my teacher.

He tells me what is right and wrong.

My drawing about how Jesus teaches me:

Jesus is so fun.

He likes to laugh and play with me.

My drawing about how fun Jesus is:

Jesus is the
best artist.

He created everything.

My drawing about how Jesus is an artist:

Jesus is my hero.

He is always helping people who need it.

My drawing about how Jesus is my hero:

Jesus is King of the whole world.

He is more powerful than anyone else.

My drawing about how Jesus is King:

Jesus is my savior.

He died on the cross for me so that when my life is done I can be together with Him in heaven.

My drawing about how Jesus is my savior:

Jesus is everlasting.

He will never go away.

My drawing about how Jesus is everlasting:

Jesus is the best!

I am very thankful for Jesus.

My drawing about how Jesus is the best:

I want to know Jesus and
be God's child forever.
I give Jesus my life today.
Amen.

My name:

_____

Written by Faytene Grasseschi - www.faytene.com
Illustrated by Michelle Vanderweir - www.michellevanderwier.com

CPSIA information can be obtained at www.ICGtesting.com
Printed in the USA
LVOW03s0615271015

459910LV00006B/13/P